中英双语版

企鹅经典 名人大发现

玛丽·居里

[美]梅根·斯泰恩(Megan Stine)◎著 [美]特德·哈蒙德(Ted Hammond)◎绘 高芸◎译

Who Was Marie Curie?

湖南科学技术出版社 小博集 BOOKY KIDS
·长沙·

著作权合同登记号：字18-2024-200

图书在版编目（CIP）数据

名人大发现. 玛丽·居里 ：汉英对照 /（美）梅根·斯泰恩（Megan Stine）著 ；高芸译 ；（美）特德·哈蒙德（Ted Hammond）绘. -- 长沙 ：湖南科学技术出版社，2025. 1. --（企鹅经典）. -- ISBN 978-7-5710-3271-5

Ⅰ. H319. 4

中国国家版本馆CIP数据核字第2024WN4978号

上架建议：科普读物

QI’E JINGDIAN · MINGREN DA FAXIAN：ZHONG-YING SHUANGYU BAN MALI JULI

企鹅经典·名人大发现：中英双语版　玛丽·居里

著　　者：［美］梅根·斯泰恩（Megan Stine）
绘　　者：［美］特德·哈蒙德（Ted Hammond）
译　　者：高　芸
出 版 人：潘晓山
责任编辑：刘　竞
策划出品：李　炜　张苗苗　文赛峰
策划编辑：马　瑄
特约编辑：杜佳美
营销编辑：付　佳　杨　朔　周晓茜
装帧设计：利　锐
内文排版：金锋工作室
出　　版：湖南科学技术出版社
（湖南省长沙市芙蓉中路416号　邮编：410008）
网　　址：www.hnstp.com
印　　刷：三河市航远印刷有限公司
经　　销：新华书店
开　　本：875 mm × 1230 mm 1/32
字　　数：101千字
印　　张：5.125
版　　次：2025年1月第1版
印　　次：2025年1月第1次印刷
书　　号：ISBN 978-7-5710-3271-5
定　　价：22.00元

若有质量问题，请致电质量监督电话：010-59096394　　团购电话：010-59320018

目 录

Contents

谁是玛丽·居里？

1903 年 11 月的一天，玛丽·居里和她的丈夫收到了一封信，邀请他们从巴黎前往瑞典会见国王和王后！玛丽将获得一枚金质奖章和一大笔奖金，并参加一场盛大的晚宴。她即将闻名于世界，她就要获得诺贝尔奖了！

她做了什么才获得这一切?

在那个几乎没有女科学家的年代，玛丽·居里成了一位科学家。事实上，那时候大多数女性连大学都没上过！玛丽和大多数女性不一样。她会说五种语言，她非常喜欢数学问题，以至于她父亲会在信中写下这些问题寄给她。她遇到了阿尔伯特·爱因斯坦——世界上最著名的科学家！她才华横溢，下定决心要成功。

玛丽因其在科学方面的贡献被授予诺贝尔奖。她发现了一种新金属！她称之为镭。

起初，玛丽甚至不知道这种新金属是什么，只知道它威力惊人。它释放能量，在黑暗中闪闪发光，发出了微弱的绿光。玛丽觉得它看起来像仙女之光。

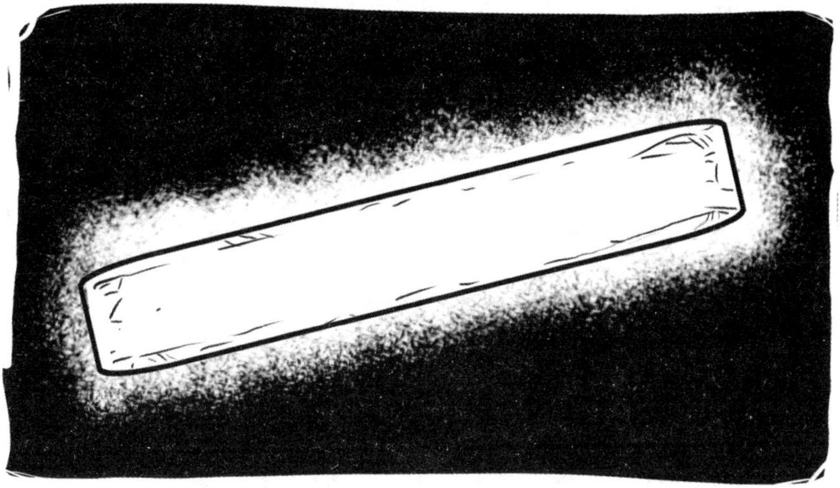

玛丽的工作完成时，她的发现将以好的和坏的方式改变世界。玛丽·居里将成为历史上最著名的女科学家。

诺贝尔奖

诺贝尔奖是最著名和最重要的奖项之一，它是由瑞典科学家阿尔弗雷德·诺贝尔创立的。阿尔弗雷德·诺贝尔发明了炸药，非常富有。为了表彰那些为人类做出杰出贡献的人，他在遗嘱中设立了诺贝尔奖。该奖项包括科学奖、医学奖、文学奖和和平奖。2013 年，每项诺贝尔奖都有一百多万美元的现金奖励！

诺贝尔奖得主会被邀请到瑞典斯德哥尔摩参加一个盛大的典礼。在那里，瑞典国王会授予他们一枚金质奖章！然后，国王和王后会举行盛大的宴会。

第一届诺贝尔奖于 1901 年颁发，其中一项科学奖颁给了威廉·伦琴，他发现了 X 射线。居里夫妇于 1903

年获得诺贝尔奖，其他著名获奖者包括阿尔伯特·爱因斯坦、马丁·路德·金、贝拉克·奥巴马、吉米·卡特和艾伯特·戈尔。

第一章

热爱学习

玛丽亚·斯克沃多夫斯卡出生于 1867 年 11 月 7 日。她排行第五，上有三个姐姐和一个哥哥。她的父母都是教师，母亲是一所学校的校长。父亲教理科，后来，他开办了自己的学校。

玛丽亚出生在波兰首都华沙。当时波兰还不是一个真正的国家，邻国占领了它，将其分成了三部分。玛丽亚住在俄罗斯帝国统治的地区。

俄国卫兵在玛丽亚居住的街道、她父母任教的学校巡逻。俄国人有严格的规定：禁止唱波兰歌曲，禁止教授波兰历史，甚至禁止学生和老师说波兰语！所有的课程都必须用俄语来教。

玛丽亚的家人讨厌俄国人，痛恨这些规定。她父亲为自己是波兰人而感到自豪，他教育孩子们热爱自己的国家。玛丽亚和她的朋友经过一座俄国人的雕像时，她们总是朝它吐唾沫！

玛丽亚是一个出色、聪明、好奇的孩子。四岁时，她喜欢盯着一个玻璃柜看，柜子里面装着父亲的科学仪器。她崇拜父亲，全神贯注地听他说的每一句话。父亲把每一次谈话都变成了一堂课。他设计了一些游戏来教孩子们地理，给他们出数学题，大声朗读诗歌。他会说五种语言，玛丽亚也学会了这五种语言。

在学校，玛丽亚是班上最聪明的孩子。她能用波兰语或俄语背诵所有正确的答案。俄国卫兵不在的时候，老师们就偷偷用波兰语授课。

一天，一个俄国卫兵来访，全班同学马上开始说俄语。大家都很紧张，如果卫兵发现了真相，可能会惩罚大家，把他们送到西伯利亚，那个地方既寒冷又遥远。

老师叫玛丽亚用俄语回答卫兵的问题，玛丽亚出色地通过了测试，但她为此感到非常难过！因为服从了俄国人的命令，她觉得自己是祖国的叛徒。

玛丽亚一家的生活很艰难，她母亲患了肺结核，病得很重。为了恢复健康，她不得不离开一年多。

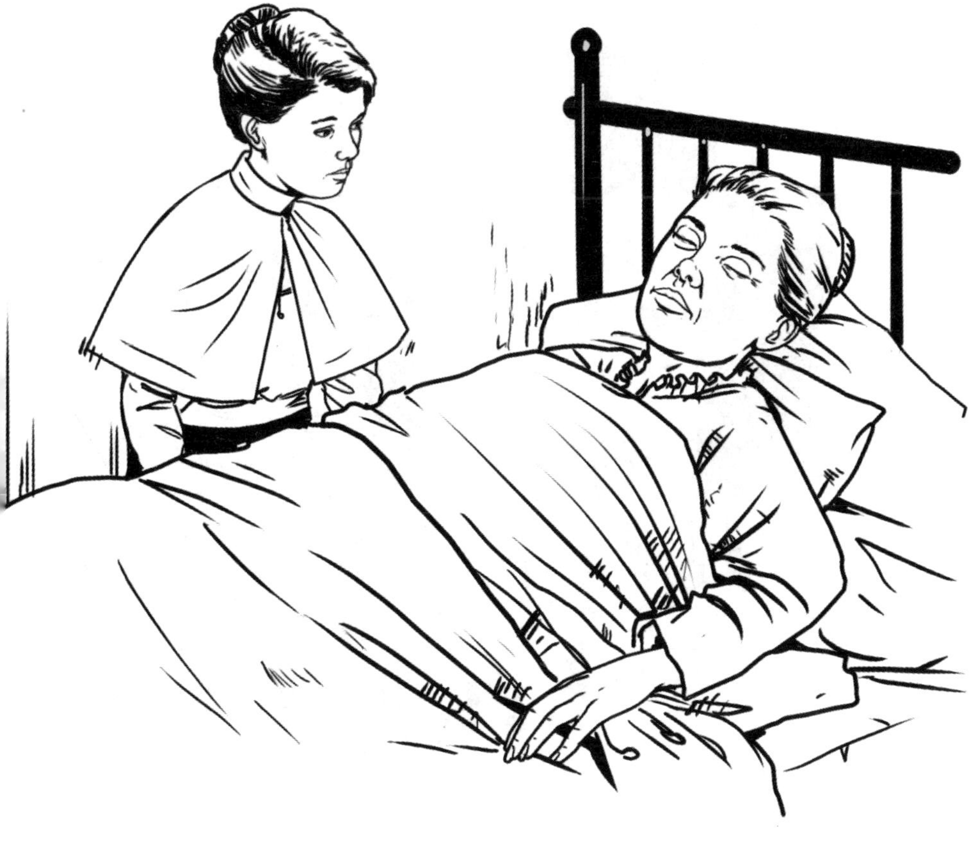

不久后，父亲被一所俄国人学校解雇了。为了赚钱，他在家里开办了一所寄宿学校。家里每天都有二十多个

男孩上课，有些孩子和他们住在一起，有些孩子只是来学习。房子拥挤、嘈杂，而且不太干净。

拥挤使人更容易生病。玛丽亚的姐姐索非娅患了斑疹伤寒，不幸去世。四年后，玛丽亚的母亲也去世了。玛丽亚非常悲伤。

学年结束时，玛丽亚的老师告诉玛丽亚的父亲，玛丽亚压力很大，应该休学一年。但她的父亲却把她送到了一所条件艰苦的俄国人学校。在玛丽亚的家里，从来没有人中断学习。

1883 年，十五岁的玛丽亚以全班第一名的成绩毕业，她甚至获得了学校最佳学生金质奖章！

中学毕业后，玛丽亚的父亲同意让女儿休息一下。玛丽亚太小，还不能结婚。父亲没有能力供她上大学，把她送到了乡下的亲戚家。

在接下来的一年里，玛丽亚过着无忧无虑的美好生活。她的叔叔们演奏音乐，带她去跳舞，邀请各种有趣的客人来家里。许多日子里，玛丽亚睡得很晚，像个孩子一样在外面玩耍。她喜欢荡秋千、采集野浆果、钓鱼、阅读和玩游戏。晚上，她去参加聚会，学习波兰的一种

名叫玛祖卡的民间舞蹈。

她觉得很自由！她后来写道，在农村，她甚至可以“唱爱国歌曲而不用坐牢”。

这是她年轻时最快乐的时光。

第二章

秘密学校

玛丽亚休息后精神焕发，年纪也够大了，她渴望上大学。但家里的钱一次只够供一个孩子上学，哥哥约瑟夫已经在医学院读书了，玛丽亚和姐姐们不得不等着轮到她们上学。此外，华沙大学不让女生入学！

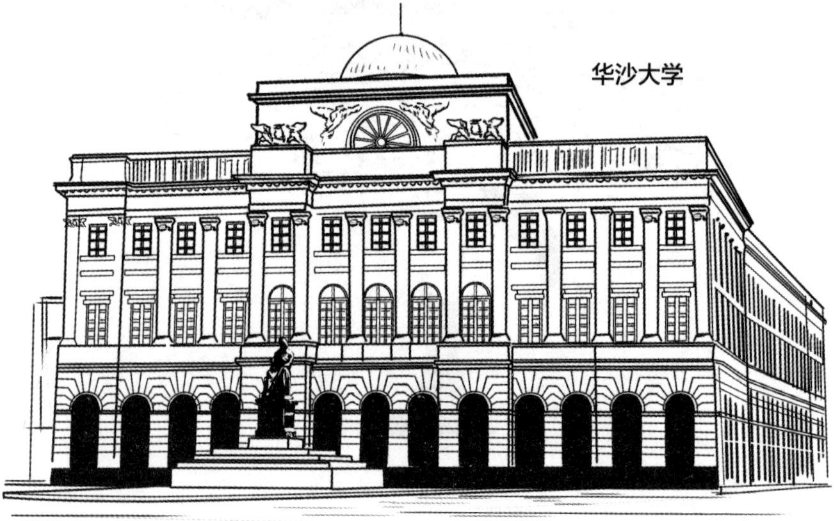

接下来的一年，玛丽亚决定独自学习，她渴望成为像父亲一样的科学家。没有老师、实验室和教室，她如何学习科学？

幸运的是，有一个非常聪明的女人可以帮忙。这个女人名叫雅德维加·达维多瓦。雅德维加知道许多年轻的波兰女性想要学习，她就开办了一所秘密大学！尽管这意味着违反了俄国的规则，要冒着受惩罚的风险。

起初，这些课程是在私人住宅中教授的，华沙最聪明的科学家和作家都自愿去授课。后来，雅德维加秘密

雅德维加·达维多瓦

地把课堂搬到了更大的建筑里。课堂必须不断迁移——从一个地方搬到另一个地方——这样俄国警察就不会发现。很快，它就被称为流动大学！

玛丽亚和她的姐姐布罗尼亚在流动大学里上课。

尽管如此，她们都梦想着有一天能上一所真正的大学，但是上哪所大学呢？最佳选择是索邦学院，它是法国巴黎的一所著名院校，也可能是欧洲最好的学校，而且招收女性。

索邦学院

玛丽亚和布罗尼亚想到了一个办法：她们轮流上学！布罗尼亚先去巴黎学习，玛丽亚留在波兰挣钱。等到布罗尼亚从索邦学院毕业后，就轮到玛丽亚上学了。

玛丽亚找了一份家庭教师的工作。十八岁时，她离开了深爱的父亲和心爱的家，去了乡下一个富裕的家庭生活。作为家庭教师，她的工作是给那个家庭的孩子们上课，其中一个女孩比玛丽亚还大一岁！

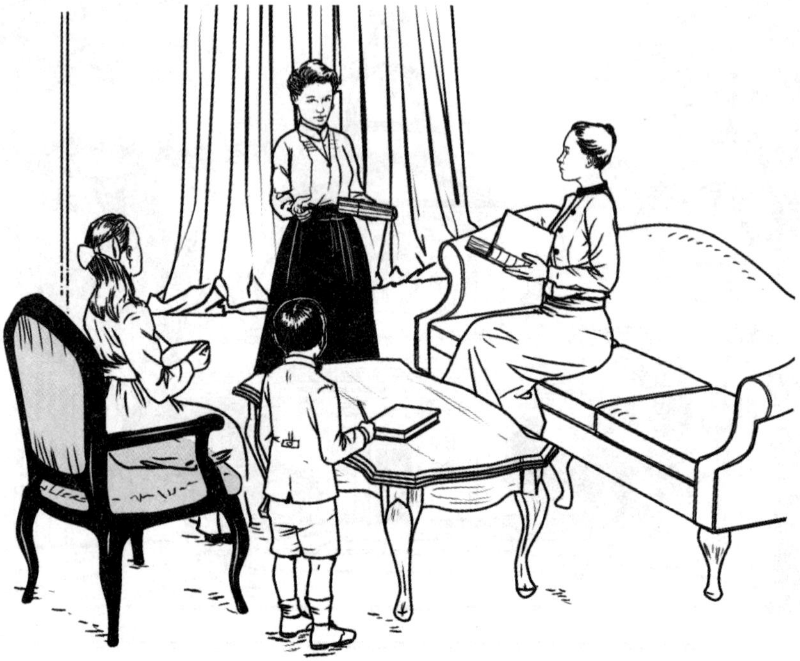

起初，玛丽亚很喜欢这份工作。她有自己的大房间，有充足的食物，孩子们的父母对她也很友善。他们邀请她参加聚会，像对待家人一样对待她。在空闲时间，她阅读数学和科学书籍。

有一天，发生了一件事，改变了一切。玛丽亚遇见了家里的长子，他名叫卡齐米日，简称卡齐。玛丽亚和卡齐相爱了，但他的家人发现后，禁止他们结婚。为什么呢？因为她只是个家庭教师！尽管她很聪明，受过良好的教育，举止得体，但他们认为她更像一个仆人，不配嫁给他们的儿子。

从那一刻起，玛丽亚就痛苦不堪。她不愿和那些瞧不起她的人一起生活，不想为他们工作，但她必须信守对布罗尼亚的承诺。她继续工作了一年或更长时间，但一直讨厌这份工作。

在那之后，玛丽亚在另一个家庭当家庭教师，然后回到家中，又在流动大学学习。

终于，她的姐姐布罗尼亚从巴黎给她来信了。布罗尼亚已经完成了学业，嫁给了卡齐米日——一个碰巧和玛丽亚的前男友同名的男人！布罗尼亚和卡齐邀请玛丽亚和他们一起生活，这样她就可以上索邦学院了。

1891 年，玛丽亚登上了开往巴黎的火车。到达后，她将开始使用一个新名字——玛丽，这是玛丽亚的法文名字。

一种全新的生活即将开始。

第三章

苦中作乐

乘火车去巴黎花了三天时间，玛丽付不起座位费，她一路上都坐在自带的凳子上！车厢里很冷，她把自己裹在毯子里。在旅途中，她几乎没有足够的食物吃。这只是她日常生活中许多困难的开始。

但是玛丽并不在乎。终于实现了自己的梦想，她非常高兴。索邦学院是一个与众不同的地方，几乎没有任何规则。她想上什么课就上什么课，如果不愿意，就可以不去上课。她甚至可以选择是否参加考试！最棒的是，学费全免。

不过，和布罗尼亚一起生活并不是那么有趣。布罗尼亚和卡齐都是医生，他们的病人

来公寓接受治疗，房子里总是拥挤嘈杂。玛丽每天去索邦学院的路程很远，她不得不冒着严寒，坐在一辆敞篷公共马车的顶层，单程就要花一个小时。

六个月后，玛丽搬了出去，在离索邦学院更近的地方租了房子。她租的公寓在顶层，只有一个小单间，没有厨房，所以她用酒精灯做饭！她的饭菜少得可怜——

只有面包，也许还有一杯热巧克力、一个鸡蛋或水果。有一次，玛丽在图书馆学习时饿得晕倒了。

冬天，她的房间非常冷，碗里的水都结冰了！如果想要取暖，就得买煤，并且将它们搬上六楼。她并不总是买得起煤，大多数时候，她睡觉时把所有的衣服都堆在身上来保暖。

对一个女人来说，独自在巴黎生活是很艰难的。当时，很少有女性上过大学。玛丽进入索邦学院科学系时，该系有一千八百二十五名学生，但其中只有二十三名是女性！在法国学习的女性太少了，法语中甚至没有“女学生”这个词，只有“学生的女朋友”这个词。

起初，玛丽会说法语，但不是太流利。为了听懂法国人讲话，并确保自己发音正确，她必须发奋努力。

尽管如此，玛丽还是很开心。多年后，她称这是她一生中最美好的回忆之一。她喜欢她的课程，把醒着的每一分钟都花在学习上。除了科学，她对任何事情都不感兴趣。全欧洲最著名的一些科学家给她授课，她的一位老师加布里埃尔·李普曼后来因发明了一种制作彩色照片的方法而获得了诺贝尔奖。

加布里埃尔·李普曼

经过三年不断地刻苦学习，玛丽参加了理科期末考试。那一年只有两名女生毕业，玛丽是全班第一名，领先于所有的男生！

既然已经完成了学业，玛丽想回波兰老家，她答应过父亲要回去照顾他。

接着幸运的事情发生了。她获得了奖学金，可以再待一年。这次她将学习数学！玛丽无法抗拒，学习是她一生中做过的最令她满意的事情。为什么她现在要停下来呢?

第四章

彼此相爱

接下来的一年里，玛丽在索邦学院学习数学。她参加考试时，得了全班第二名！

现在她是不是该像她承诺的那样回波兰呢？

还不是。玛丽的老师加布里埃尔·李普曼帮她在索邦学院的实验室里找了一份工作，她的任务是研究磁力和钢铁。

磁力是使磁铁和金属吸在一起的力。这份工作对玛丽来说再好不过了——做实验总是最快乐的事。只有一个问题——实验室里没有最好的设备，玛丽在实验中遇到了很大的困难，不能得到好的结果。

皮埃尔·居里

为了帮助玛丽，一些波兰朋友把她介绍给一个名叫皮埃尔·居里的法国人。皮埃尔是一位科学家，在很年轻的时候就出名了。皮埃尔二十一岁时，他和他的哥哥发现石英晶体可以携带电荷。之后，他发明了一种叫静电计的科学工具，可以用来测量非常小的电量。玛丽需要他的静电计做实验。

从遇见皮埃尔的那天起，玛丽的整个人生都发生了改变。在那之前，她一直以为自己再也不会坠入爱河了。她认为这无关紧要，打算将自己的一生完全奉献给科学。

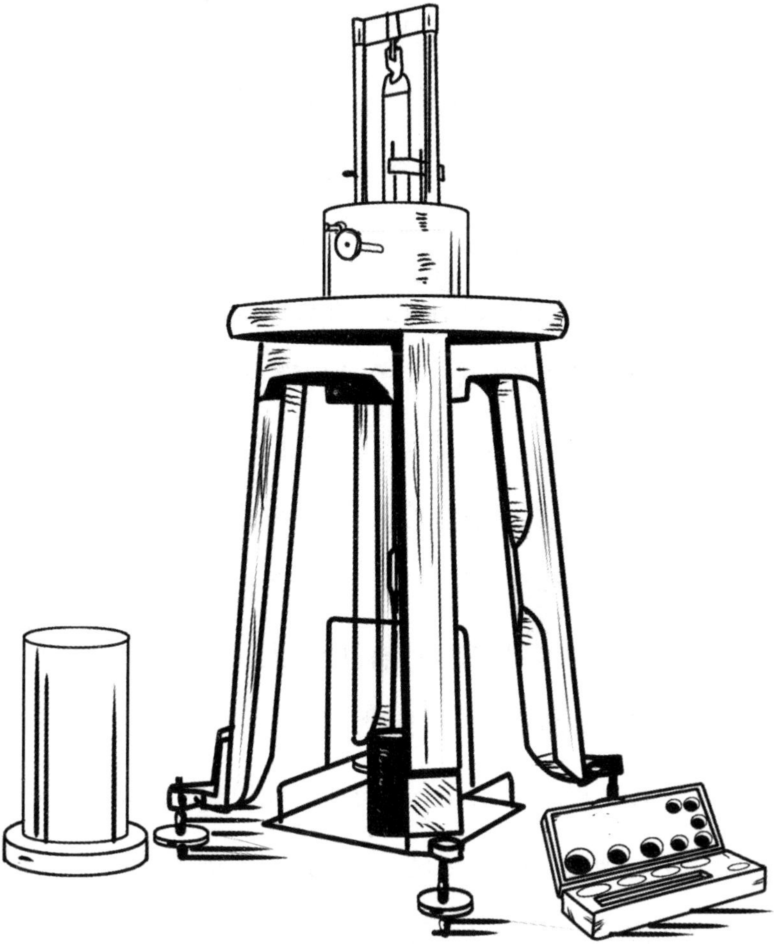

但是皮埃尔太特别了，与其他男人太不一样了。他聪明、安静，和她一样热爱科学。在很多方面，他都很像玛丽。

皮埃尔也是在一个和玛丽一样的家庭中长大的。他的父亲是医生，也是科学家。他的父母认为教育极其重要——就像玛丽的父母一样。与玛丽不同的是，皮埃尔在学校学习有困难，所以他的父母在家里教他，让他找寻自己的路。当他发现自己非常喜欢数学和科学时，他从一个学习迟缓者变成了一个才思敏捷的人。

皮埃尔二十三岁的时候，已经在大学教书了！

玛丽和皮埃尔相遇的那一刻，彼此就知道对方很特别。皮埃尔觉得自己找到了一个“天才女人”，玛丽认为皮埃尔是那种可以交谈和信任的男人。她邀请他到她的小房间里一边品茶，一边探讨科学。

很快，皮埃尔就爱上了玛丽。他想和她结婚，但玛丽还不太确定。1894 年夏天，她回到了华沙的家。卡齐曾经伤透了她的心，她还没做好再爱一次的准备。

然而，皮埃尔并没有放弃。他写信给她，恳求她回巴黎和他在一起。他甚至提出离开法国——一个他所热爱的国家，去波兰和她一起生活。

最后，玛丽意识到皮埃尔真的很爱她，作为科学家，他们可以一起生活。1895 年 7 月 26 日两人在法国结婚。在一个天气极好的夏日，婚宴在皮埃尔父母的花园里举行。美味佳肴齐上桌，包括一只巨大的火鸡和一些大桃

子！用餐后，客人们在草坪上玩了一场法式球类游戏。无论从哪方面来说，这都是一个快乐的时刻。

为了度蜜月，他们买了两辆自行车，开始了漫长的冒险之旅。他们的蜜月骑行之旅持续了一整个夏天！

秋天回到巴黎后，他们很快就开始工作了。没有什么比整天甚至整夜待在实验室里更让他们开心的了。

第五章

新的发现

在接下来的几年里，玛丽一直在学习，并继续从事磁力研究工作。

与此同时，她很享受和皮埃尔在一起的生活。她每周都会买鲜花回家，学会了用醋栗做果冻。她和皮埃尔骑着自行车到处走，他们越来越相爱了。

1897年9月12日，玛丽和皮埃尔有了一个女儿，他们给她取名伊雷娜。

孩子几个月大的时候，皮埃尔的父亲搬来和他们一起住。他的妻子刚刚去世，他孤身一人，愿意帮忙照顾孙女。玛丽很高兴，因为她乐意回去工作。

在那个年代，女性几乎从不外出工作。但玛丽不一样，她想做一些重要的研究，这样她就能获得博士学位，

这个学位可以让她成为一位老师。

现在唯一的问题是：她应该研究什么？

玛丽和皮埃尔在巴黎度过了一段激动人心的时光。全世界都在为一项新的科学发现——X射线而疯狂！神秘的X射线是两年前才被发现的，科学家们正试图弄清楚X射线究竟是如何工作的。他们很快注意到X射线可以使一些东西在黑暗中发光。

但是玛丽想研究自己的课题，她决定研究另一种射线——贝可勒尔射线。这种射线是以其发现者亨利·贝可勒尔的名字命名的，来自一种叫铀的金属。

今天，我们知道铀是能释放强放射性射线的几种金属之一。但玛丽·居里开始研究时，放射性这个词甚至还不存在！没有人知道为什么铀会释放能量，也没有人知道它为什么能让物质在黑暗中发光。当时没有人知道铀可以用来制造炸弹或核电站，玛丽的研究将为所有这些知识打开大门。

玛丽在皮埃尔的帮助下建立了一个两人共用的实验

亨利·贝可勒尔

亨利·贝可勒尔出身于一个科学家家庭，他的父亲和祖父都是科学家。他们研究磷光物质——在黑暗中发光的东西。

亨利跟随他们的脚步。他没做多少工作，很快就被法国科学院录取了。他父亲很有名，所以亨利很容易成功。

亨利用X射线和铀做实验，他比玛丽·居里更早发现了放射性，但贝可勒尔没有使用“放射性”这个词。他没有意识到很多化学物质可以释放能量，也没有完全明白能量从何而来。贝可勒尔坚持认为能量与磷光有关。

在第一次成功后，亨利停止了对铀的实验，这也是玛丽·居里决定接手的原因之一。

室，它只是皮埃尔任教的学校里的一间旧储藏室，又冷又脏。但玛丽并不介意，她只关心工作。

在实验室里，玛丽用皮埃尔的静电计测量来自不同金属的射线。测试非常棘手，她的手必须非常稳当。没有人能比玛丽做得更好，就连贝可勒尔也尝试过，但他失败了！

起初，玛丽测试了铀。然后她测试了其他金属，包括金和铜，只有铀会发出射线。

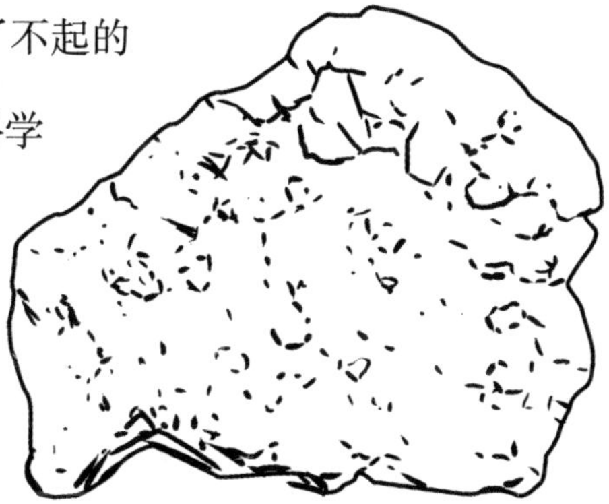
沥青铀矿

接着玛丽做了一件了不起的事——一件永远改变了科学的事，她决定测试一种叫沥青铀矿的岩石。沥青铀矿是一种含有大量铀的岩石，但它也含有其他金属。

玛丽测试沥青铀矿时，发现它发出的射线甚至比单独的铀还要多！这怎么可能呢？玛丽找到了答案。一定有其他东西——另一种金属——混合在沥青铀矿里！另一种金属，不管它是什么，它比铀的能量还要大。

玛丽很快就明白了真相，她发现了一种全世界都不知道的新元素！

玛丽以她的祖国波兰的名字给这种新金属命名，称之为钋。然后她想出了一个词来形容金属发出的射线——“放射性”，这意味着像钋和铀这样的金属能够向空气中释放能量。

什么是元素?

世界上每一种“纯”化学物质都被称为元素[①]。铜、金、铀等金属是元素,氦气球内的气

① 元素:化学上指具有相同核电荷数(即相同质子数)的同一类原子的总称,如氧元素、铁元素。

元素周期表

1 氢								
3 锂	4 铍							
11 钠	12 镁							
19 钾	20 钙	21 钪	22 钛	23 钒	24 铬	25 锰	26 铁	27 钴
37 铷	38 锶	39 钇	40 锆	41 铌	42 钼	43 锝	44 钌	45 铑
55 铯	56 钡	57–71	72 铪	73 钽	74 钨	75 铼	76 锇	77 铱
87 钫	88 镭	89–103	104 𬬻	105 𬭊	106 𬭳	107 𬭛	108 𬭶	109 鿏
镧系元素		57 镧	58 铈	59 镨	60 钕	61 钷	62 钐	63 铕
锕系元素		89 锕	90 钍	91 镤	92 铀	93 镎	94 钚	95 镅

体——氦也是元素。我们呼吸的空气不是元素，因为它不是单一的“纯”化学物质，而是氧和其他元素的混合物。

科学家们有一张图表，里面有世界上所有的已知元素。到目前为止，我们已经知道了一百一十八种，但科学家们仍有可能发现更多的元素。

								2 氦
			5 硼	6 碳	7 氮	8 氧	9 氟	10 氖
			13 铝	14 硅	15 磷	16 硫	17 氯	18 氩
28 镍	29 铜	30 锌	31 镓	32 锗	33 砷	34 硒	35 溴	36 氪
46 钯	47 银	48 镉	49 铟	50 锡	51 锑	52 碲	53 碘	54 氙
78 铂	79 金	80 汞	81 铊	82 铅	83 铋	84 钋	85 砹	86 氡
110 𫟼	111 𬬭	112 鿔	113 鿭	114 𫓧	115 镆	116 𫟷	117 石田	118 鿫
64 钆	65 铽	66 镝	67 钬	68 铒	69 铥	70 镱	71 镥	
96 锔	97 锫	98 锎	99 锿	100 镄	101 钔	102 锘	103 铹	

为了让世界知道她的新发现，玛丽做了科学家们通常会做的事情：她写了一份报告，想把它读给巴黎科学院的其他科学家听。

巴黎科学院就像一个高级科学俱乐部，聚集了法国最重要的科学家。它很难加入，成员必须通过投票产生。

玛丽和皮埃尔都不是巴黎科学院的成员。那时，皮埃尔甚至找不到一份在索邦学院教书的工作！其他科学家认为玛丽和皮埃尔不够优秀，因为他们没有获得名牌大学的博士学位。此外，玛丽是个女人。巴黎科学院从不让女性进入，女性甚至不允许进入巴黎科学院的房间！

不过幸运的是，玛丽和皮埃尔有极具影响力的朋友。欧美所有著名的科学家都彼此认识。1898 年 4 月，玛丽的老师和朋友加布里埃尔·李普曼向科学院宣读了她的报告。

科学家们对玛丽的报告很感兴趣，但是没有人感到惊讶——至少当时还没有。他们不确定她是否正确，玛丽还是得证明钋的存在。那怎么办呢？只有把它从沥青铀矿中分离出来。

她必须抓紧时间！既然全世界都知道了钋，其他科学家可能也想研究它，就连贝可勒尔也对玛丽的工作感兴趣。那个时代，就像今天一样，科学家们试图互相帮助，但他们也相互竞争，都想成为第一个提出新想法的人。

贝可勒尔对玛丽来说既是朋友又是竞争对手。他帮助玛丽筹集了一些钱做实验，但他并没有告诉她钱的事，而是告诉了皮埃尔！他认为她没有皮埃尔重要，因为她是个女人。贝可勒尔也从玛丽的工作中汲取了灵感，试

什么是放射性?

放射性是一种特殊的能量，它来自某些金属或化学物质的原子内部。当某物具有放射性时，它会释放出能量射线，直到能量全部消耗殆尽。

放射性金属需要多长时间才能失去所有的能量？答案“因金属而异”。有些金属在几分钟、几小时或几天内迅速失去能量。有些金属，比如镭，需要很长时间才能失去能量。科学家们用“半衰期”来描述元素失去一半能量所需的时间。镭的半衰期约为一千六百年，这意味着镭需要数千年才能失去所有的能量。

一旦能量耗尽，金属就不再危险了。

图自己做类似的实验。

皮埃尔则完全相反。他不喜欢竞争，只是热爱科学本身。玛丽踌躇满志，想为自己的发现赢得赞誉。她决心成为证明新金属存在的第一人。

玛丽开始工作了。她试图把钋从沥青铀矿中分离出来，但没有成功，沥青铀矿中钋的含量太少了。

然而，就在她尝试的时候，她无意中发现了别的东西。更好的东西！沥青铀矿中含有另一种发出射线的神秘金属，它甚至比钋更具放射性。那是什么？

玛丽做了一系列测试来寻找答案。经过几次实验，她意识到自己发现了另一种新元素！她和皮埃尔把这种新金属命名为镭。镭的威力非常大，即使是最小量的镭，其放射性也是铀的一百万倍。

对玛丽和皮埃尔来说，这是令人惊奇的一年。到1898年12月，她已经发现了两种不为世人所知的新化学元素！其他科学家开始注意到她的工作。

然而，一些科学家仍然想要更多的证据，他们不确定她是否正确。他们想亲眼看看镭，亲手摸摸镭。

有没有可能把镭从沥青铀矿中分离出来呢?

玛丽决定试一试。

第六章

它会发光

玛丽现在小有名气，她希望科学界能对她表示一些尊重。她和皮埃尔想要一个有新设备的洁净空间，于是请求索邦学院提供一个更大更好的实验室，这样她就可以继续工作了。

但索邦学院拒绝了。

他们说她可以接管学院附近的一栋旧建筑，这栋建筑又大又脏，还漏水，曾被医学院的学生用来解剖尸体做实验！

她的实验室里没有暖气，冬天冷得要命。玛丽和皮埃尔只好一边喝茶，一边蜷缩在一个小火炉旁取暖。

有些日子里，玛丽因为工作太忙而忘了吃饭。有些晚上，她回家看望女儿，但在伊雷娜睡着后又回到了实

验室。

长达三年的时间里，玛丽筛选了数吨沥青铀矿。这是一项艰苦的工作。碎石被送到实验室外的院子里，她在一个巨大的容器里搅拌着大量的棕色粉末和其他化学

物质。她必须把混合物煮沸，然后冲洗以分离出金属。冲洗一吨碎石需要五十吨水！玛丽总共用了八吨沥青铀矿和四百吨水才完工！

渐渐地，玛丽成功了，她从沥青铀矿中提取出了微量的镭。起初它不是纯镭，只是一种叫镭盐的物质。但她一直在努力，试图得到一种更纯净的金属。

镭盐每晚在黑暗的实验室里都会发出可爱的光，玛丽和皮埃尔把一个装有镭盐的玻璃罐带回家，放在床边，他们喜欢看它在黑暗中发光。

接触镭不是一个好主意，但玛丽当时并不知道。镭发出的射线很危险，触摸它会损伤皮肤，虽然速度很慢。亨利·贝可勒尔在夹克里随身携带了一管镭盐，几周后，靠近镭管的皮肤被灼伤了。皮埃尔发现同样的事情也发

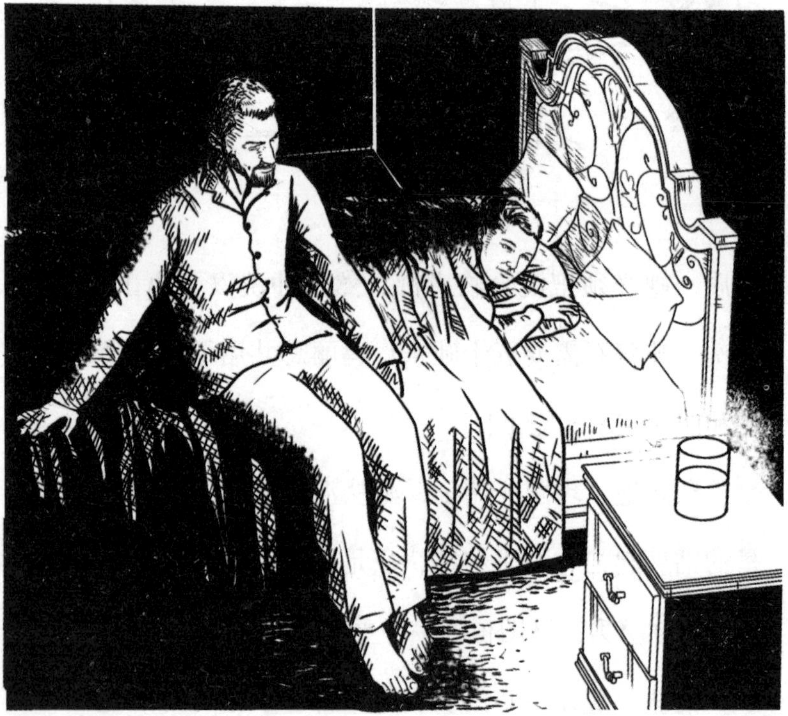

生在他自己身上。待在镭的周围也会损害他们的身体，使他们生病。

尽管如此，玛丽仍然坚持工作，并撰写有关她的发现的研究报告。有时她和皮埃尔一起写，但他们仍然没有得到充分的尊重。贝可勒尔通常会受到更多的关注和敬重。和贝可勒尔竞争着工作一定很艰难，尤其是当皮埃尔认为贝可勒尔在暗地里阻止他进入科学院的时候。

1902 年 7 月，将近四年后，玛丽终于得到了几粒纯镭！这足以证明它确实存在。其他科学家对这种金属进行了测试，并同意了她的观点。

玛丽又写了一篇关于她的发现的长篇研究论文，有了这份报告，她现在可以获得索邦学院的博士学位了。玛丽从不在乎穿着，但她为这个场合买了一件新衣服。1903 年 6 月，她举行了一次庆祝晚宴。除了皮埃尔，还有几个朋友和著名科学家出席了宴会，其中包括加布里埃尔·李普曼，他们都为她感到骄傲。

现在，玛丽和皮埃尔希望他们能得到好工作，能在

分光镜：如何识别新金属

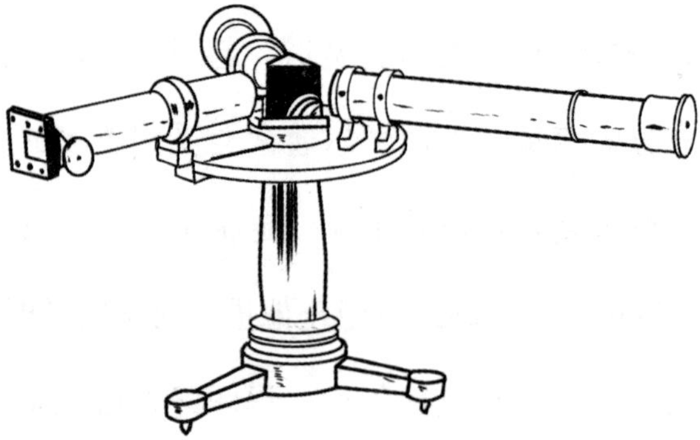

每一种化学元素都是独一无二的。金属也是如此，因为金属是化学元素。

为了识别一种化学物质，科学家们将其加热到足以使其发光的程度。然后他们用一种叫分光镜的工具来观察亮光，分光镜可以使人看到从亮光中发出的彩虹图案。光的彩虹图案被称为光谱。

每种元素发出的光都有其独特的图案或光谱——有点像指纹。如果科学家看到了一种他们从未见过的图案，他们就知道这是一种全新的元素！

玛丽·居里发现镭时，尽管她看不见它，但她知道这种金属的存在！证明它存在的唯一方法就是把镭放在分光镜下。玛丽花了三年多的时间才得到足够的镭来进行测试。

一个像样的实验室里工作，他们只想要一个既干净又安静的工作场所。但他们即将收到更令人兴奋的消息，他们就要获得诺贝尔奖了！

第七章

名利双收

诺贝尔奖是当今科学家所能获得的最高荣誉。玛丽和皮埃尔收到来信，得知他们获得了诺贝尔奖。然而信中并没有透露太多细节，没有提及瑞典国王会亲自颁奖，也没有告知他们将获得一大笔奖金——在今天价值超过五十万美元！

于是皮埃尔做了一件令人震惊的事。他给诺贝尔奖委员会回信，说他们不能去领奖！他感谢他们的奖励，并解释说玛丽生病了。他说，旅程太长了，他们正忙于上课，不可能花时间去瑞典。

皮埃尔和玛丽可能没有意识到自己的无礼，也不知道诺贝尔奖有多重要，该奖项只颁发了三年。

居里夫妇本应与另一位科学家亨利·贝可勒尔一同

获得诺贝尔奖。贝可勒尔去了瑞典领奖，他发表演讲时，说得好像所有的工作都是他一个人做的一样，几乎没有提到玛丽和皮埃尔。

尽管如此，居里夫妇还是一夜成名，所有的报纸都在报道他们。人们被玛丽——一位女科学家迷住了！报社记者日复一日地来到她家，玛丽不在时，记者们采访

了她的女儿伊雷娜。他们甚至写了关于她的猫的故事！

报上称玛丽为“居里夫人”。在某种程度上，他们是在说玛丽只是皮埃尔·居里的妻子——她自己并不出名。玛丽在余生中都被称为居里夫人。

皮埃尔讨厌这种宣传，讨厌任何妨碍他工作的事情。几周以来，玛丽和皮埃尔都试图避开记者。当被问问题时，他们只简单地回答“是”或者“不是”。

他们的名气带来了一件好事，现在索邦学院愿意给皮埃尔一份教学的工作。此外，经过多年的请求，他和玛丽终于有了一个更好的实验室。

与此同时，全世界都爱上了镭。为什么呢？因为它在黑暗中闪闪发光！对许多人来说，这种光芒就像一种神奇的药剂。人们认为它能治病——他们在一定程度上是对的。镭可以帮助治疗癌症，但反过来说，镭也会让人生病，包括玛丽和皮埃尔。

有钱人每天傻乎乎地喝镭水，直到他们的下颌骨碎成碎片！演员和舞者在他们的服装上涂上镭，这样他们就能在黑暗中闪闪发亮。把镭涂在钟表上，这样指针就会发光。一家化妆品公司甚至在他们的口红里放了镭！所有这些镭产品都在伤害人们。

镭对玛丽和皮埃尔的伤害最大，因为他们接触了这么多年。皮埃尔的手严重受损，甚至不能自己穿衣服。他的骨头疼

痛，难以行走。

玛丽也经常感到虚弱。但到了 1904 年，她身体很健康，可以再生一个孩子了！ 12 月 6 日，一个女婴出生了，他们给她起名夏娃。

在获得诺贝尔奖后的几个月里，玛丽和皮埃尔享受着生活。他们去海滨度假，用奖金买新衣服，在外面吃丰盛的大餐。大部分钱都寄给了玛丽在波兰的家人。生活似乎很美好。

1906 年 4 月的一天，一件可怕的事情发生了，这件事彻底改变了玛丽的生活。

第八章

悲惨境遇

1906 年 4 月 19 日，天下着雨，整个巴黎阴沉沉、湿漉漉的。那天早上，皮埃尔出去参加一个科学会议。他心情很好，他的朋友说他比以前更快乐，话也更多了。

会议结束后，皮埃尔冒雨回去，外面到处都是马、马车、汽车、人和有轨电车。皮埃尔穿过一条繁忙的大街时，一辆巨大的马车撞上了他。皮埃尔试图抓住马，

使自己站稳，但他虚弱无力，摔倒了。车夫无法使沉重的马车停下来，车轮从皮埃尔身上碾过，碾碎了他的颅骨。

几个小时后，玛丽听到丈夫去世的噩耗。这对她的打击，就像杀死皮埃尔的那辆马车一样沉重。玛丽觉得好像再也没有快乐的理由了，她变得沉默不语，不吃不喝，几乎不下床。在她看来，她的生命似乎结束了。

好几个月里，玛丽都很痛苦和孤独。她后来写道，她的孩子伊雷娜和夏娃是她活下去的唯一理由。

过了一段时间，索邦学院邀请玛丽接替皮埃尔的教学工作，玛丽同意了，但这是一个苦乐参半的胜利。皮埃尔在世的时候，他们不让她当老师！因为从来没有女

性在索邦学院教过书。现在皮埃尔去世了，他们欢迎她接替他的位置。

1906 年 11 月的一天，玛丽第一次来上课，数百人站在街道两旁。记者和摄影师都来了，人群等着听著名的居里夫人说些什么。她会提到皮埃尔吗？会谈论他对

科学界有多重要吗？没有。玛丽只是从皮埃尔中断的地方开始上科学课。即便如此，人群中还是有人哭了，他们都能体会到玛丽的感受。没有他的日子，对她来说有多么艰难！

在接下来的几年里，玛丽一直很悲伤。尽管如此，她还是继续工作，并把家搬到了离巴黎不远的乡间的一所房子里。玛丽希望伊雷娜和夏娃能在户外游泳和玩耍，她也想让她们学习。伊雷娜特别聪明，和玛丽一样喜欢数学和科学，夏娃擅长音乐。

玛丽和她的朋友们在家里给一小群孩子上课。这有点像流动大学，所有的成年人轮流在彼此的家里授课。

玛丽的朋友都是科学家。他们一起吃饭，一起教孩子，一起去海滩度假，关系非常亲密。

一天，朋友们注意到玛丽的变化。突然间，她似乎更快乐了！她再也没有穿黑衣悼念皮埃尔，而是穿了一条带花的漂亮裙子。

很快，她的朋友就找出了玛丽快乐的原因。她坠入爱河了！唯一的问题是，她所爱的男人——保罗·朗之万——已经结婚了。

保罗·朗之万

保罗是玛丽和皮埃尔朋友圈子的一员。他曾是皮埃尔的学生，是一位杰出的科学家和好朋友。保罗的婚姻很不幸，有时他的妻子很暴力，保罗真希望未曾娶她。

玛丽可能从没想过自己会爱上一个已婚男人，但她还是遵从自己的内心，和他在一起。这是她多年来第一次感到幸福。

保罗给玛丽写情书，玛丽也给他回信。一天，保罗的妻子让娜发现了这些信件，她怒不可遏，扬言要杀了玛丽！她甚至在街上跟踪玛丽！

玛丽试图说服保罗离婚。保罗和让娜有四个孩子，他不想拆散家庭。最后，他向妻子保证，他不会再见玛丽——只和她做朋友。

那一年，玛丽即将再次创造历史，她被提名为法国科学院首位女院士。法国准备好平等对待女性了吗？支持和反对的两方反应都很强烈。许多报纸对此发表了充满愤怒的文章，有人认为不应该允许女性加入这个由男性科学家组成的私人团体。尽管玛丽已经是世界上最著名的科学家之一，但他们认为应该把她拒之门外。

到了投票的时候，玛丽甚至不被允许进入学院的大

楼去看看发生的一切！

投票于 1911 年 1 月 24 日四点整进行。玛丽没有当选，她的朋友对此很生气，但玛丽表现得毫不在乎，她不是那种对任何事情都大惊小怪的人。

况且，玛丽还有工作，并且她仍然爱着保罗。

1911 年 11 月，玛丽去比利时布鲁塞尔参加一个非常重要的科学会议。欧洲所有最著名的科学家都在那里，包括阿尔伯特·爱因斯坦，保罗·朗之万也去了。

保罗的妻子发现保罗和玛丽都在布鲁塞尔时，非常愤怒。她怀疑保罗和玛丽仍然相爱，于是把玛丽的情书寄给了巴黎的报社！一桩可怕的丑闻爆发了，报纸上每天都有关于玛丽和保罗的报道，许多法国人认为玛丽应受到谴责。

玛丽又气又怕，她不想让自己的女儿受到负面报道的影响，也不想因此毁了自己的事业。

对这种麻烦来说，这是个很糟糕的时机。就在这一周，玛丽刚刚收到诺贝尔奖委员会的一封信。他们又给了她一个诺贝尔奖！这一次，她单独获奖。这是一个了不起的荣誉！

玛丽害怕报纸上的报道会毁掉诺贝尔奖，她的担忧并没有错。

几周后，诺贝尔奖委员会又给她寄来了一封信。在所有报纸报道了那些故事之后，他们希望玛丽拒绝领奖！他们请求她不要来斯德哥尔摩。

玛丽不想错过这个创造历史的机会。她告诉委员会，她的私生活与工作无关，她要去斯德哥尔摩领奖。玛丽认为他们只是给她颁发诺贝尔科学奖，其他都无关紧要。

1911 年 12 月，玛丽和瑞典国王坐在房间里，国王授予她一枚纯金奖章，玛丽高昂着头发表了演讲。宴会上有洋蓟、鱼、鸡肉和葡萄酒，她的女儿伊雷娜和她的姐姐布罗尼亚也在那里分享她的喜悦。

对她们所有人来说，这都是一次激动人心的经历，十四岁的伊雷娜将对此终生难忘。但这不会是伊雷娜最后一次专程去斯德哥尔摩。

第九章

科学世家

对玛丽来说，第二次获得诺贝尔奖一定是一件很美妙的事，但是与保罗·朗之万的可怕丑闻对她造成了很大的影响。她在各方面都疲惫不堪——生病、悲伤、沮丧，镭的毒害可能仍然使她身体虚弱，而且她还患有其他疾病。

在接下来的几年里，玛丽躲了起来。她和保罗的恋情结束了，但世人不会因此原谅她。人们朝她的窗户扔石头，报纸不停地报道她的绯闻。

玛丽无法忍受人们说的那些坏话，她到处旅行，把孩子交给家庭教师照顾。无论走到哪里，玛丽都用假名，她不想让别人知道她是谁。如果有人认出她，问道："你是居里夫人吗?"她会撒谎说不是。

最后，玛丽和一个好朋友在英国休息了很长时间后，感觉好多了。她回到巴黎，重新开始工作。

随着时间的推移，人们忘记了这桩丑闻。她又一次能够做自己，做她的工作。伊雷娜也长大了，她和玛丽成了搭档。她们一起谈论科学，就像玛丽和皮埃尔一样。

1914 年，为了玛丽的研究，一整栋大楼建立起来。起初它被称为镭研究所，但后来更名为居里研究所。玛丽希望她和伊雷娜能很快在那里一起工作。

在实验室启用之前，第一次世界大战爆发了。德国人入侵了法国。玛丽想帮忙，她决定要做的第一件事就是把法国所有的镭都带走并藏起来！她不想让德国人发现镭。

玛丽把镭放在一个沉重的手提箱里，坐了十个小时的火车，把镭存放在波尔多一所大学的地下室里，然后她回到巴黎，这过程中她一天半没吃东西。没有什么事情比她执行任务更重要。

接下来，玛丽发明了一种小型 X 光机，运送方便，给受伤的士兵使用。这种设备被称为“小居里”，玛丽和十七岁的伊雷娜开车把设备送到战场附近的医院。

第一次世界大战

第一次世界大战始于1914年，奥匈帝国打响了第一枪。很快，欧洲的许多国家开始相互争斗。法国、英国和俄国是同一条战线，与德国和奥匈帝国打仗。德国人是进攻者，他们进军比利时和法国，想要接管政权。

1917年，美国加入战争，帮助拯救英国和法国。四百多万美国人在欧洲与德国人打仗。美国、英国和法国打败了德国，取得了胜利。战争于1918年11月11日结束。

四年后，德国战败，伊雷娜回到巴黎继续她的学业。最终，她毕业了，成了一位科学家，和玛丽一起工作。

后来有一天，保罗·朗之万以一种奇特的方式回到了她们的生活中。保罗告诉玛丽，他的一个年轻学生名叫弗雷德里克·约里奥，这个学生非常崇拜玛丽和皮埃尔·居里，想在玛丽的实验室里工作。

弗雷德里克·约里奥

玛丽给了他一份工作，很快弗雷德里克就爱上了伊雷娜。起初，玛丽不信任弗雷德里克，以为他只是想接近著名的居里家族，但最终她还是喜欢上了他。伊雷娜和弗雷德里克·约里奥于 1926 年 10 月 9 日结婚。

玛丽一直觉得镭可以用来治疗癌症，她是对的。她在余生致力于研究用镭来帮助人们的方法。与此同时，她的女儿和弗雷德里克也做了他们自己的研究。他们发现了“人工放射性”！随着玛丽年龄的增长和病情的加重，伊雷娜接管了镭研究所。

1934 年 5 月，玛丽又开始感到非常虚弱。镭最终取得了胜利，她生命垂危。她的女儿夏娃带她去法国的山区休息，但无济于事。玛丽于7月4日去世，享年六十六岁。

玛丽所有的衣服、书籍、笔记本和私人物品都很危险，不能触碰。它们有放射性！她在实验室里用的所有东西都受到了镭的影响。事实上，即使过了一百年，她的东西仍然具有放射性，处理起来也不安全！

玛丽去世后，被安葬在皮埃尔长大的那个法国小村庄里，长眠在皮埃尔身侧。

伟大的居里家族的名气并没有就此结束，就在第二年，伊雷娜和弗雷德里克·约里奥因为在化学方面的发现而获得了诺贝尔奖。

伊雷娜和弗雷德里克有两个孩子——埃莱娜和皮埃尔，他们长大后也都成了科学家。令人惊讶的是，埃莱

娜嫁给了保罗·朗之万的孙子，他也是一位科学家！

玛丽的小女儿夏娃不是科学家，她成了一位作家。她写了一本关于她母亲的书，名叫《居里夫人》，她的书使玛丽在美国名声大噪。

直到今天，玛丽仍然是科学界最著名的女性。许多建筑物都以她的名字命名，两个博物馆专门展示她的生活和工作，她的肖像被印在法国和波兰的货币上。

1995 年，法国决定挖出玛丽和皮埃尔的灵柩，并将其移葬先贤祠。先贤祠是巴黎的一座古老的建筑，里面安葬着法国最著名的人物。法国总统出席了这个盛大的仪式。

最终，玛丽·居里是一位女性的事实并不重要，她终于得到了最高的尊重和应得的荣誉。她的工作改变了世界，她的名字将流传千古。

玛丽·居里生平年表

1867 年	玛丽亚·斯克沃多夫斯卡出生于波兰。
1883 年	十五岁时以高中第一名的成绩毕业。
1891 年	赴巴黎索邦学院求学。
1895 年	与皮埃尔·居里结婚。
1897 年	长女伊雷娜出生。
1898 年	发现了两种新的化学元素。
1902 年	获得纯镭的样品。
1903 年	因其在放射性方面的工作，与皮埃尔一起获得诺贝尔奖。
1904 年	皮埃尔开始在索邦学院任教。
	第二个女儿夏娃出生。
1906 年	皮埃尔在一次事故中丧生。
	接替皮埃尔在索邦学院的教学工作。
1911 年	第二次获得诺贝尔奖。
1914 年	在第一次世界大战期间，发明了 X 光机来帮助战场上受伤的士兵。
1926 年	女儿伊雷娜和弗雷德里克·约里奥结婚。
1934 年	六十六岁去世。

世界大事年表

1863年	首条客运地铁在伦敦开通。
1865年	亚伯拉罕·林肯总统遇刺身亡。
1869年	苏伊士运河通航。
1876年	亚历山大·格雷厄姆·贝尔发明了电话。
1883年	经过十多年的建设，布鲁克林大桥通车。
1903年	首批无声电影之一《火车大劫案》上映。
	莱特兄弟驾驶第一架飞机。
1908年	亨利·福特推出T型车。
1912年	泰坦尼克号沉没。
1914年	第一次世界大战在欧洲爆发。
	巴拿马运河完工。
1917年	美国加入第一次世界大战。
1919年	《凡尔赛和约》签署，标志着第一次世界大战正式结束。
1929年	美国股市大崩盘，引发经济大萧条。
1931年	帝国大厦竣工。
1932年	阿梅莉亚·埃尔哈特成为第一位独自飞越大西洋的女飞行员。

Who Was Marie Curie?

One day in November 1903, Marie Curie and her husband got a letter in the mail. The letter invited them to travel from Paris to Sweden to meet the king and queen! Marie was about to be given a gold medal, a fancy dinner, and a huge amount of money. She was about to become famous all over the world. She was about to win the Nobel Prize!

What had she done to deserve all this?

Marie Curie was a scientist at a time when there were almost no female scientists. In fact, most women didn't even go to college then! Marie wasn't like most women. She spoke five languages. She loved math problems so much that her father sent them to her in his letters. She met Albert Einstein—the most famous scientist in the world! She was brilliant and determined to succeed.

The Nobel Prize

The Nobel Prize is one of the most famous and important awards given. It was created by the Swedish scientist who invented dynamite. Alfred Nobel was very rich. He wanted to reward people who helped make the world a better place. He created the Nobel Prize in his will. The prizes are given for sciences, medicine, literature, and peace. In 2013, each Nobel Prize came with a cash award of more than $1 million!

The winners of the Nobel Prize are invited to come to Stockholm, Sweden, for a fancy ceremony. There, they are given a gold medal by the King of Sweden! Then a huge banquet is held with the king and queen.

The very first Nobel Prizes were given in 1901. One of the science prizes was given to Wilhelm Röntgen, the man who discovered X-rays. Marie and Pierre Curie won in 1903. Other famous winners include Albert Einstein, Martin Luther King Jr. , Barack Obama, Jimmy Carter, and Al Gore.

Marie was being given the Nobel Prize for her work in science. She had discovered a new metal! She called it radium.

At first, Marie didn't even know what this new metal was. All she knew was that it was amazingly powerful. It gave off energy! It glowed in the dark, giving off a faint green light. Marie thought it looked like fairy light.

By the time her work was done, Marie's discovery would change the world in good ways and bad. Marie Curie would be the most famous woman scientist in history.

Chapter 1

Eager to Learn

Maria Sklodowska was born on November 7, 1867. She was the youngest of five children, with three older sisters and one brother. Her parents were both teachers. Her mother was the principal of a school. Her father taught science. Later, he ran his own schools.

Maria was born in Warsaw, the capital city of Poland. Poland didn't really exist as a country at that time. The neighboring countries had taken over Poland and divided it up into three parts. Maria lived in the part that was ruled by Russia.

Russian guards walked the streets where Maria lived, and patrolled the schools where her parents taught. The

Russians had strict rules. No one could sing Polish songs. Schools weren't allowed to teach Polish history. Students and teachers couldn't even speak Polish! All the classes had to be taught in Russian.

Maria's family hated the Russians and hated the rules. Her father was very proud to be Polish. He taught his children to love their country. When Maria and her friend walked past a Russian statue, they spat on it!

Maria was a wonderful, bright, and curious child. At age four, she loved to stare into a glass case that held her father's science equipment. She adored her father and listened intently to everything he said. Her father turned every conversation into a lesson. He created games to teach his children geography. He gave them math problems. He read poems aloud. He spoke five languages, and Maria learned to speak them, too.

At school, Maria was the smartest girl in her class. She could recite all the right answers in either Polish or Russian.

When the Russian guards weren't around, the teachers were sneaky. They taught classes in Polish.

One day a Russian guard came to visit. Quickly, the whole class switched back to speaking Russian. Everyone felt nervous. If the guards found out the truth, they might punish people. They might send them away to a cold, distant place in Russia called Siberia.

The teacher called on Maria to answer questions in Russian for the guard. Maria passed the test brilliantly, but she felt bad for doing it! She felt like a traitor to her country for obeying the Russians.

Life was hard for Maria's family. Her mother was very sick with a disease called tuberculosis. She had to go away for more than a year to try to get well.

Soon after, her father was fired from his job at a Russian school. To make money, he started a boarding school at home. More than twenty boys came each day. Some of them lived with the family. Others just came to study. The house was crowded, noisy, and not very clean.

The crowding made it more likely that people would get sick. Maria's sister Zofia got a disease called typhus and died. Four years later, Maria's mother died. Maria became deeply sad.

At the end of the school year, Maria's teacher told her father that Maria was stressed out. The teacher thought Maria should take a year off from school. Instead, her father sent her to a tough Russian school. In Maria's family, no one ever took a break from learning.

In 1883, Maria graduated first in her class at the age of fifteen. She even got the school's gold medal for being the best student!

After high school, Maria's father agreed to let his daughter have a break. Maria was too young to get married, and her father could not afford to send her to college. Instead, he sent her to live with relatives in the countryside.

For the next year, Maria lived a wonderful, carefree life.

Her uncles played music, took her to dances, and invited all kinds of interesting guests to the house. Many days, Maria slept late and then played outside like a child. She loved swinging, collecting wild berries, fishing, reading, and playing games. At night she went to parties and learned a Polish dance called the mazurka.

She felt so free! In the countryside, she later wrote, she could even "sing patriotic songs without going to prison."

It was the happiest time she had ever had in her young life.

Chapter 2

The Secret School

Rested and older now, Maria was eager to start college, but there was only enough money in the family for one student at a time. Her brother Jozef was already in medical school. Maria and her sisters would have to wait their turns. Besides, Warsaw University didn't let girls in!

For the next year, Maria decided to study on her own. She longed to be a scientist like her father. How would she ever learn science without teachers and laboratories and classrooms?

Luckily, there was a very clever woman who could help. The woman's name was Jadwiga Dawidowa. Jadwiga knew that many young Polish women wanted to study, even if it meant risking punishment and breaking the Russian rules. Jadwiga started a secret university!

At first, the classes were taught in private homes. The smartest scientists and writers in Warsaw volunteered to teach. Later, Jadwiga secretly moved the classes to bigger buildings. The classes had to keep moving—flying from place to place—so the Russian police wouldn't find out. Soon it became known as the Flying University!

Maria and her sister Bronia took classes at the Flying University.

Still, they both dreamed of attending a real university someday, but where? The best choice was the Sorbonne, a famous university in Paris, France. It was probably the best school in Europe, and it accepted women.

Maria and Bronia came up with a plan. They would take turns! Bronia would go to Paris first to study. Maria would stay in Poland to earn money for them both. After Bronia graduated from the Sorbonne, it would be Maria's turn.

Maria took a job as a governess. At the age of eighteen, she left her beloved father and home behind to live with a rich family in the countryside. Her job as governess was to teach the children in that family. One of her students was a girl a year older than Maria!

At first, Maria liked the job. She had her own big room. There was plenty of food and the parents were kind to her. They invited her to parties and treated her almost like a member of the family. In her free time, she read math and science books.

One day, something happened that changed everything. Maria met the oldest son in the family. His name was Kazimierz, or Kaz for short. Maria and Kaz fell in love, but when his family found out, they forbade him to marry her. Why? Because she was only a governess! Even though she was smart, educated, and had good manners, they thought she was more like a servant. She wasn't good enough to marry their son.

From that moment on, Maria was miserable. She hated living and working for people who looked down on her, but she had to keep her pledge to Bronia. For another year or more, she kept the job, hating it all the time.

After that, Maria worked as a governess for another family, then she returned home to study at the Flying University again.

Finally her sister Bronia wrote to her from Paris. Bronia had finished her schooling and had married a man who happened to have the same name as Maria's old boyfriend—Kazimierz! Bronia and her Kaz invited Maria to come live with them so she could attend the Sorbonne.

In 1891, Maria boarded a train for Paris. When she arrived, she would begin to use a new name—Marie. It was the French version of Maria.

A whole new life was about to begin.

Chapter 3

Hungry But Happy

The train trip to Paris took three days. Marie couldn't pay for a seat. She rode the whole way on a stool that she brought with her! The train car was so cold, she kept herself wrapped in blankets. She barely had enough food to eat during the trip. It was just the first of many hardships that would soon be part of her everyday life.

Marie didn't care, though. She was happy to be finally fulfilling her dream. The Sorbonne was such a different kind of place. There were almost no rules. She could take whatever classes she wanted. She didn't have to attend class if she didn't feel like it. She could even choose whether or not to take tests! Best of all, the tuition was free.

Living with Bronia was not so much fun, though. Bronia and Kaz were both doctors. Their patients came to the apartment for treatment. The house was always crowded and noisy. Marie's trip to the Sorbonne every day was a long one. She had to ride in the cold, on the top deck of an open bus, an hour each way.

After six months, Marie moved out and rented her own place closer to the Sorbonne. Her apartment was a tiny single room on the top floor of an apartment building. She had no kitchen, so she did all her cooking over an alcohol lamp! Her meals were skimpy—just bread with maybe a cup of hot chocolate, an egg, or fruit. One time, Marie was so hungry that she fainted while studying in the library.

In winter, her room was so cold that water would freeze in a bowl! If she wanted heat, she had to buy coal and carry it up six flights of stairs. She couldn't always afford coal. Most of the time she slept with all her clothes piled on top of her, to keep warm!

It was a hard time for a woman to live alone in Paris. Very few women went to college. When Marie entered the science department at the Sorbonne, there were 1,825 students—but only twenty-three of them were women! There were so few women studying in France that the French didn't even have a word for "female student." The only word they had meant "girlfriend of a student."

Marie spoke French but not very well at first. She had to work hard to understand French people and to make sure she pronounced words correctly.

Still, Marie was happy. Years later, she called it one of the best memories of her life. She loved her classes, and spent every waking minute studying. She didn't care about anything except science, and she was being taught by some of the most famous scientists in all of Europe. One of her professors, Gabriel Lippmann, would later win a Nobel Prize for inventing a way to make color photographs.

After three years of hard work and constant study, Marie

took her final exams in science. Only two women graduated that year. Marie was first in her whole class—ahead of all the men!

Now that she was finished studying, Marie thought she would go home to Poland. She had promised her father to come back and take care of him.

Then something lucky happened. She got a scholarship to stay another year. This time she would study math! Marie couldn't resist. Learning was the most satisfying thing she had ever done in her life. Why would she want to stop now?

Chapter 4

Two Loves

For the next year, Marie studied math at the Sorbonne. When she took her exams, she came in second in the class!

Was it time now to go back to Poland as she had promised?

Not quite yet. Marie's professor, Gabriel Lippmann, found her a job in a lab at the Sorbonne. Her task was to study magnetism and steel.

Magnetism is the force that causes magnets and metal to stick together. It was perfect for Marie—she was always happiest doing experiments. There was only one problem—the lab didn't have the best equipment. Marie struggled with her experiments. She couldn't get good results.

To help her, some friends from Poland introduced Marie

to a Frenchman named Pierre Curie. Pierre was a scientist who had become famous at a very young age. When Pierre was twenty-one, he and his brother had discovered that quartz crystals could hold an electrical charge. After that, he invented a scientific tool called an electrometer. It was used to measure very small amounts of electricity. Marie needed his electrometer for her experiments.

The day Marie met Pierre, her whole life changed. Until then, she had thought she would never fall in love again. She thought it didn't matter. She was planning to devote her life solely to science. But Pierre was so special, so different from other men. He was smart, quiet, and he loved science as much as she did. In so many ways, he was just like Marie.

Pierre had been brought up in a family just like Marie's, too. His father was a doctor and scientist. His parents thought education was extremely important—just like Marie's. Unlike Marie, Pierre had had trouble learning in school, so his parents taught him at home. They let him find his own way.

When he discovered how much he liked math and science, he went from being a slow learner to being super fast.

By the time Pierre was twenty-three years old he was teaching college!

The minute Marie and Pierre met, they each knew that the other was special. Pierre felt he had found a "woman of genius." Marie knew that Pierre was the kind of man she could talk to and trust. She invited him to her tiny room to discuss science and sip tea.

Very soon, Pierre was in love with Marie. He wanted to marry her, but Marie was not so sure. In the summer of 1894, she went home to Warsaw. Her heart had been broken once by Kaz. She wasn't ready to take another chance on love.

Pierre wouldn't give up, though. He wrote to her and begged her to come back to Paris to be with him. He even offered to leave France—a country he loved—and come live in Poland.

Finally Marie realized Pierre truly loved her and that

they could have a life together as scientists. The two of them were married in France on July 26, 1895. On a perfect summer day, the wedding reception was held in his parents' garden. Wonderful food was served, including a huge turkey and giant peaches! After they ate, the guests played a French ball game on the lawn. It was a happy occasion in every way.

For their honeymoon, they bought two bicycles and rode off on a long adventure. Their honeymoon bike trip lasted all summer long!

When they came back to Paris in the fall, they quickly got to work. Nothing made them happier than spending all day—and even all night—in a lab.

Chapter 5

Marie's Discovery

For the next few years, Marie kept studying. At the same time, she kept her job doing research in magnetism.

Meanwhile, she enjoyed her life with Pierre. She bought fresh flowers each week for their apartment. She learned to make jelly from gooseberries. She and Pierre rode their bicycles everywhere. They fell more and more in love.

On September 12, 1897, Marie and Pierre had a baby girl. They named her Irene.

When the baby was a few months old, Pierre's father moved in with them. His wife had just died, and he was alone. He was willing to help take care of his granddaughter. Marie was glad because she was ready to get back to work.

In those days, women almost never worked outside of the home, but Marie was different. She wanted to do some important research so that she could get her PhD—the degree that would make her a professor.

The only question now was: What should she work on?

Marie and Pierre lived during an exciting time in Paris. The whole world was going crazy for a new scientific discovery—X-rays! The mysterious X-rays had just been discovered two years earlier. Scientists were trying to figure out how X-rays really worked. They soon noticed that X-rays could make some things glow in the dark.

But Marie wanted to study a topic of her own. She decided to study a different kind of rays, called Becquerel rays. These rays were named for Henri Becquerel, the man who discovered them. The rays came from a metal called uranium.

Today we know that uranium is one of several metals that give off powerful radioactive rays. But when Marie

Henri Becquerel

Henri Becquerel came from a family of scientists. Both his father and his grandfather were scientists. They had studied things that were phosphorescent—things that glowed in the dark.

Henri followed in their footsteps. Without doing much work, he was quickly admitted to the French Academy of Sciences. Because Henri's father was famous, Henri had an easy path to success.

Henri experimented with X-rays and uranium. He discovered radioactivity before Marie Curie did, but Becquerel didn't use the word radioactivity. He didn't realize that lots of chemicals could give off energy, and he didn't completely understand where the energy was coming from. Becquerel held on to the idea that the energy had something to do with phosphorescence.

After his first success, Henri stopped experimenting

with uranium. That's one reason Marie Curie decided to pick it up.

Curie started her research, the word *radioactive* didn't even exist! No one knew why uranium gave off energy or why it could make things glow in the dark. No one knew then that uranium could be used to make a bomb or a nuclear power plant. Marie's research was going to open the door for all that knowledge.

Marie set up a laboratory with Pierre's help. They shared the lab together. It was cold and grungy—just an old storage room in the school where Pierre taught. Marie didn't mind. Work was all she cared about.

In the lab, Marie used Pierre's electrometer to measure rays coming from different metals. The tests were very tricky. She had to have very steady hands. No one else could do the tests as well as Marie. Even Becquerel had tried and failed!

At first, Marie tested uranium. Then she tested other metals, including gold and copper. Only the uranium gave off rays.

Then Marie did something brilliant—something that

would change science forever. She decided to test a rock called pitchblende. Pitchblende is a rock that contains a lot of uranium. But it has other metals in it, too.

When Marie tested the pitchblende, she found it gave off even *more* rays than uranium alone! How could that be? Marie figured out the answer. There had to be something else—another metal—mixed into the pitchblende! That other metal, whatever it was, had even more energy than uranium.

Soon Marie realized the truth. She had discovered a new element that the world didn't know about!

Marie named the new metal after her homeland of Poland. She called it polonium. Then she came up with a word for the rays that the metals gave off. She called it "radioactivity." It meant that metals like polonium and uranium were able to release energy into the air.

To let the world know about her new discoveries, Marie did what scientists always do: She wrote a report. She wanted to read it to a group of other scientists in the Academy of

What Is an Element?

Every pure chemical in the world is called an element. Metals such as copper, gold, and uranium are all elements. So are gases such as helium—the gas inside helium balloons. The air we breathe is not an element because it isn't a single, pure chemical. Air is a mixture of oxygen and other elements.

Scientists have a chart that tells them what all the elements in the world are. So far, we know of 118 elements, but scientists still could discover more.

Sciences in Paris.

The Academy was like a fancy science club for the most important scientists in France. It was hard to join and members had to be voted in.

Marie and Pierre were not members of the Academy. At that time, Pierre couldn't even get a job teaching at the Sorbonne! Other scientists thought Marie and Pierre weren't good enough because they didn't have PhDs from the best colleges. Besides, Marie was a woman. The Academy never let women in. Women weren' t even allowed inside the Academy's rooms!

Luckily, though, Marie and Pierre had important friends. All the famous scientists in Europe and America knew one another. In April 1898, Marie's report about her discoveries was read to the Academy by her teacher and friend Gabriel Lippmann.

The scientists were interested in Marie's report, but no one was amazed—not yet. They weren't sure she was right.

What Is Radioactivity?

Radioactivity is a special kind of energy that comes from inside the atoms in certain metals or chemicals. When something is radioactive, it gives off energy rays until the energy is all gone.

How long does it take for a radioactive metal to lose all its energy? The answer differs for each metal. Some metals lose energy quickly—in only a few minutes, hours, or days. Other metals, like radium, can take a very long time to lose their energy. Scientists use the term "half-life" to describe how long it takes for an element to lose half of its energy. Radium has a half-life of about 1,600 years. That means it takes thousands of years for radium to lose all its energy.

Once the energy is gone, the metal isn't dangerous anymore.

Marie still had to prove that polonium existed. How? By separating it out of the pitchblende.

She had to hurry! Now that the world knew about polonium, other scientists might want to study it. Even Becquerel was interested in Marie's work. In those days, just like today, scientists tried to help one another, but they also competed with one another to be the first with new ideas.

Becquerel was both a friend and a competitor. He helped Marie get some money for her experiments, but instead of telling Marie about the money, he told Pierre! He treated her like she wasn't as important as Pierre because she was a woman. Becquerel also took ideas from Marie's work and tried to do similar experiments himself.

Pierre was totally the opposite. He didn' t like to compete. He simply loved science for its own sake. Marie was the ambitious one. She wanted credit for her discovery. She was determined to be first to prove that her new metal existed.

Marie got to work. She tried to separate the polonium from the pitchblende—but she failed. The amounts of polonium in the pitchblende were too tiny.

While she was trying, though, she stumbled onto something else. Something even better! The pitchblende contained another mysterious metal that was giving off rays. This one was even more radioactive than polonium. What was it?

Marie did a series of tests to find out. After several experiments, she realized she had found another new element! She and Pierre named this new metal radium. Radium was so powerful that even the tiniest amount was a million times more radioactive than uranium.

It was an amazing year for Marie and Pierre. By December 1898, she had discovered two new chemical elements that the world hadn't known about! Other scientists were beginning to notice her work.

However, some scientists still wanted more proof. They

weren't sure she was right. They wanted to see the radium, and touch it.

Was it even possible to separate the radium from the pitchblende?

Marie was determined to try.

Chapter 6

It Glows!

Now that Marie was a little bit famous, she hoped the scientific world would show her some respect. She and Pierre asked the Sorbonne for a bigger, better laboratory. They wanted a clean space with new equipment so she could continue her work.

The Sorbonne refused.

Instead, they said she could take over a huge, dirty, leaky, old building near the college. The building had been used by medical students to cut up dead bodies for experiments!

There was no heat in her lab. In the winter, the place was horribly cold. Marie and Pierre had to huddle around a small stove to keep warm, sipping cups of tea.

Some days Marie forgot to eat, she was so busy with her work. Some nights, she went home to see her daughter, but then went back to her lab after Irene was asleep.

For three long years, Marie sifted through tons of pitchblende. It was backbreaking work. The crushed rocks were delivered to the courtyard outside her lab. She stirred huge amounts of brown dust in a giant pot with other chemicals. She had to boil the mixture, then wash it to separate out the metals. It took fifty tons of water to wash one ton of crushed rocks! All together, Marie used eight tons of pitchblende and four hundred tons of water before she was done!

Little by little, Marie was succeeding. She was getting tiny amounts of radium out of the pitchblende. At first it wasn't pure radium. It was just something called radium salts, but she kept working, trying to get a purer form of the metal.

The radium salts gave off a lovely glow each night in the dark lab. Marie and Pierre brought a glass jar of it home to keep beside their bed. They liked to watch it glow in the dark.

Marie didn't know it at the time, but handling radium wasn't a good idea. The rays it gave off were dangerous. Touching it damaged her skin, although slowly. Henri Becquerel had carried a glass tube of radium salts around in his jacket. A few weeks later, his skin was burned in the spot where the radium had been. Pierre found the same thing happened to him. Being around radium damaged the insides of their bodies, too. It was making them sick.

Still, Marie kept working and writing research reports about her discoveries. Sometimes she and Pierre wrote them together. Marie and Pierre were still not fully respected. Often, Becquerel was given more attention and respect. It must have been hard to work side by side with Becquerel, especially when Pierre thought that Becquerel was secretly trying to keep him out of the Academy of Sciences.

Finally in July 1902, after nearly four years, Marie had a few grains of pure radium! It was enough to prove it really existed. Other scientists tested the metal and agreed she was right.

Marie wrote another long research paper about her discovery. With this report, she could now get her PhD from the Sorbonne. Marie had never cared about clothes, but she bought a new dress for the occasion. In June 1903, she had a celebration dinner. Besides Pierre, several friends and famous scientists joined her, including Gabriel Lippmann. They were all so proud of her.

Now Marie and Pierre hoped that they would both be able to get good jobs with a decent laboratory. That's all they wanted: a clean, quiet place to work. But they were about to receive something even more exciting. They were about to win the Nobel Prize!

Spectroscopes: How New Metals Are Identified

Every pure chemical element is unique. This is true for metals, too, because metals are chemical elements.

To identify a chemical, scientists heat it up enough to make it glow. Then they look at the glowing light with a tool called a spectroscope. A spectroscope can see a rainbow pattern of colors coming from the glowing light. The rainbow pattern of light is called a spectrum.

The glow from every element creates its own unique pattern or spectrum—sort of like a fingerprint. If scientists see a pattern they've never seen before, they know it's a brand-new element!

When Marie Curie discovered radium, she knew the metal existed, even though she couldn't see it! The only way to prove it existed was to put the radium under a spectroscope. It took Marie more than three years to get enough radium for the test.

Chapter 7

Fame and Fortune

The Nobel Prize is the highest honor a scientist can receive today. However, when Marie and Pierre received the letter saying they had won, it didn't give them very many details. It didn't say the king of Sweden would be there to hand out the award, and it didn't tell them that they would be getting a huge amount of money—worth more than half a million dollars today!

So Pierre did something shocking. He wrote back to the Nobel Prize committee and said they couldn't come! He thanked them for the prize and explained that Marie was sick. The trip was too long, he said. They couldn't possibly take the time to travel to Sweden. They were too busy teaching their classes.

Pierre and Marie probably didn't realize they were being rude. They also didn't know what a big deal the Nobel Prize was. The prize had only been around for three years.

The Curies were supposed to share the Nobel Prize with one other scientist, Henri Becquerel. Becquerel went to Sweden and accepted the award instead. When he gave his speech, he made it sound like he had done all the work. He hardly mentioned Marie and Pierre at all.

Still, the Curies became famous overnight. All the newspapers wrote about them. People were fascinated by Marie—a woman scientist! Newspaper reporters came to her house day after day. When Marie wasn't home, the reporters talked to her daughter, Irene. They even wrote stories about the cat!

The newspapers called Marie "Madame Curie." In a way, they were saying that Marie was only Pierre Curie's wife—not famous on her own. Marie was known as Madame

Curie for the rest of her life.

Pierre hated the publicity. He hated anything that kept him from his work. For weeks, Marie and Pierre tried to avoid the reporters. When asked questions, they answered with just single words. "Yes." "No."

One good thing came out of their fame. Now the Sorbonne was willing to give Pierre a job as a professor. Also, after all their years of begging, he and Marie were finally given a better lab.

Meanwhile, the whole world was falling in love with radium. Why? Because it glowed in the dark! The glow seemed like a magic potion to many. People imagined it would cure illnesses—and they were partly right. Radium could help treat cancer, but the opposite was also true. Radium was making people sick, including Marie and Pierre.

Rich people foolishly drank radium water every day until their jawbones broke into pieces! Actors and dancers put radium on their costumes so they would glow in the dark.

Radium was painted on watches and clocks so the hands would glow. One makeup company even put radium in their lipstick! All these radium products were hurting people.

Radium hurt Marie and Pierre most of all because they handled it for so many years. Pierre's hands were so damaged that he couldn't even dress himself. His bones ached. Pain made it hard for him to walk.

Marie was often weak, too. But by 1904, she was healthy enough to have another baby! On December 6, a baby girl was born. They named her Eve.

For several months after winning the Nobel Prize, Marie and Pierre enjoyed life. They took vacations to the seashore. They bought some new clothes with their prize money, and ate a few fancy dinners out. Big chunks of the money were sent to Marie's family in Poland. Life seemed good.

Then one day in April 1906, something terrible happened—something that turned Marie's life upside down forever.

Chapter 8

Misery

It was rainy, gray, and damp all over Paris on April 19, 1906. Pierre had gone out to a science meeting that morning. He was in a wonderful mood. His friends said he was happier and talked more than ever before.

After the meeting, Pierre went back out into the rain. There were horses, carriages, cars, people, and trams everywhere. As Pierre began to cross a big, busy street, a huge horse-drawn wagon hit him. Pierre tried to grab on to the horse, to steady himself, but he was weak. He fell. The wagon driver couldn't stop the heavy cart. The wheel ran over Pierre and crushed his skull.

A few hours later, Marie heard the terrible news that her

husband was dead. It struck her as hard as the wagon that killed Pierre. Marie felt as if there was no reason to be happy ever again. She became silent. She wouldn't eat and barely got out of bed. It seemed to her as if her life was over.

For many months, Marie was miserable and alone. She later wrote that her children, Irene and Eve, were her only reasons to go on living.

After a while, the Sorbonne invited Marie to take over Pierre's teaching job. Marie agreed, but it was a bittersweet triumph. While Pierre was alive, they would not let her be a professor! No woman had ever taught at the Sorbonne. Now that Pierre was dead, she was welcome to take his place.

On the November day in 1906 when Marie arrived to teach her first class, hundreds of people lined the streets. Reporters and photographers came. The crowds waited to hear what the famous Madame Curie would say. Would she mention Pierre? Would she talk about how much he meant to the world of science? No. Marie simply began the science lesson where Pierre had left off. Even so, people in the audience cried. They all sensed how Marie felt, and how hard it was for her to go on without him.

For the next few years, Marie was sad. Still, she continued her work and moved her children to a house in the country, not far from Paris. Marie wanted Irene and Eve to be able to swim and play outside. She also wanted them to learn. Irene was especially smart and, like Marie, loved math and science. Eve was good at music.

Marie arranged with her friends to teach a small group of their children at home. It was something like the Flying University! All the adults took turns teaching classes in one another's houses.

Marie's friends were all scientists. They all spent time together, having dinner and teaching the children. They went on vacation to the beach together. They were very close.

One day, her friends noticed a change in Marie. Suddenly, she seemed happier! She was wearing a pretty dress with a flower, instead of the black dresses she had been wearing to mourn Pierre.

Pretty soon, her friends figured out why Marie was happy. She had fallen in love! The only problem was that the man she loved—Paul Langevin—was already married.

Paul was part of Marie and Pierre's circle of friends. He had been Pierre's student. He was a brilliant scientist and a good friend. Paul was unhappily married. Sometimes his wife was violent. Paul wished he hadn't married her.

Marie probably never wanted to fall in love with a married man. But she followed her heart and spent time with him anyway. It was the first happiness she had felt in years.

Paul wrote love letters to Marie, and she wrote back to him. One day, Paul's wife, Jeanne, found the letters. She was furious. She threatened to kill Marie! She even followed Marie in the street!

Marie tried to convince Paul to leave his wife and get a divorce. Paul had four children with Jeanne. He didn't want to break up his family. Finally, he promised his wife that he wouldn't see Marie again—except as a friend.

That year, Marie was on the verge of making history—again. She was nominated to become the first woman member of the French Academy of Sciences. Was France ready to treat women equally? There were strong feelings on both sides. Many newspapers wrote angry articles about it. They thought women should not be allowed into this private group of male scientists. Even though Marie was already one of the most famous scientists in the world, they thought she should be kept out.

When it came time to vote, Marie was not even allowed inside the Academy's building to see what happened!

The vote was held at exactly four o'clock on January 24, 1911. Marie was not elected. Her friends were angry about it, but Marie acted like she didn't care. She was not the kind of person to make a fuss about anything.

Besides, Marie still had her work, and she was still in

love with Paul.

In November 1911, Marie went to a very important science meeting in Brussels, Belgium. All the most famous scientists from Europe were there, including Albert Einstein. Paul Langevin went, too.

When Paul's wife found out he and Marie were in Brussels together, she was furious. She suspected that Paul and Marie were still in love. She sent Marie's love letters to the Paris newspapers! A terrible scandal broke out. There were stories about Marie and Paul in the newspaper every day. Many French people thought Marie was to blame.

Marie was angry and horrified. She didn't want her daughters to suffer from the bad publicity. She didn't want it to ruin her career, either.

It was an especially bad time for this kind of trouble. That same week, Marie had just gotten a letter from the Nobel Prize committee. They were giving her *another* Nobel Prize! This time, she alone would be the winner. It was an amazing honor!

Marie was afraid that the newspaper stories would somehow spoil the Nobel Prize. She was right.

A few weeks later, the Nobel Prize committee sent her a second letter. After all the newspaper stories, they wanted Marie to refuse the prize! They asked her not to come to Stockholm.

Marie was not going to miss out on this chance to make history. She told the committee that her private life was private. She was coming to Stockholm and accepting the prize. Marie believed they were giving her the Nobel Prize for science—nothing else. Nothing else should matter.

In December 1911, Marie sat in a room with the king of Sweden. The king gave her the solid gold medal. Marie held her head high and made a speech. A fancy banquet was served with artichokes, fish, chicken, and wine. Her daughter Irene and her sister Bronia were there to share her joy.

It was a thrilling experience for them all, and fourteen-year-old Irene would remember it all her life. It wouldn't be the last time Irene would make that special trip to Stockholm.

Chapter 9

A Family of Scientists

Winning her second Nobel Prize must have been wonderful for Marie, but the terrible scandal with Paul Langevin had taken a toll on her. She was worn out in every way—sick, sad, and depressed. The radium poisoning was probably still making her weak. She had other illnesses, too.

For the next few years, Marie went into hiding. Her love affair with Paul was over, but the world wouldn't forgive her for it. People threw stones at her windows. The newspapers kept writing stories about her.

Marie couldn't bear all the bad things people were saying. She traveled from place to place, leaving her children behind with a governess. Marie used fake names wherever she went. She didn't want people to know who she was. If someone recognized her and asked, "Are you Madame Curie?" she would lie and say no.

Finally, after a long rest in England with a good friend, Marie felt better. She went back to Paris and back to work.

As time passed, people forgot about the scandal. Once again, she was able to just be herself and do her work. Irene was growing up, too. She and Marie were becoming partners. They talked about science together, just like Marie and Pierre had.

In 1914, a whole building was built for Marie's research. At first it was called the Radium Institute, but later it was renamed the Curie Institute. Marie hoped that she and Irene would work there together very soon.

Before the lab opened, World War I broke out. The Germans invaded France. Marie wanted to help. She decided her first job was to take all the radium in France and hide it! She didn't want the Germans to find it.

Marie put the radium in a heavy suitcase and traveled ten hours by train. She stored the radium in a vault at a college in Bordeaux. Then she returned to Paris, having eaten nothing for a day and a half. When Marie was on a mission, nothing else mattered.

Next, Marie invented a small X-ray machine that could easily be carried to wounded soldiers. Her machines were called "Little Curies." Marie and seventeen-year-old Irene drove the machines to hospitals near the battlefields.

Four years later, after Germany lost the war, Irene went back to her studies in Paris. Eventually she graduated and became a scientist, working alongside Marie.

Then one day, Paul Langevin came back into their lives in a strange way. Paul told Marie about a young student of his named Frederic Joliot. Frederic idolized Marie and Pierre Curie. He wanted to work in Marie's lab.

Marie gave him a job, and soon Frederic fell in love with Irene. At first, Marie didn't trust Frederic. She thought he was just trying to get close to the famous Curie family, but eventually she came to like him. Irene and Frederic Joliot were married on October 9, 1926.

Marie had always suspected that radium could be used to treat cancer, and she was right. She spent the rest of her years working on ways to use radium to help people. At the same time, her daughter and Frederic did their own research. They discovered artificial radioactivity! As Marie grew older and sicker, Irene took over the Radium Institute.

In May 1934, Marie began to feel very weak again. The radium was finally winning out. She was dying. Her daughter Eve took her to the mountains in France, to rest, but it didn't help. Marie died on July 4 at the age of sixty-six.

All of Marie's clothes, books, notebooks, and personal things were too dangerous to touch. They were radioactive! Everything she used in the lab had been affected by the radium. In fact, even after a hundred years, her things were still so radioactive that it wasn't safe to handle them!

World War I

The first World War began in 1914. It started when Austria-Hungary fired the first shots. Pretty soon, many countries in Europe were fighting one another. France, England, and Russia were all on the same side. They fought against Germany and Austria-Hungary. The Germans were the attackers, marching into Belgium and France to take over.

In 1917, the United States joined the war to help save England and France. More than four million Americans fought the Germans in Europe. America, England, and France won, defeating Germany. The war ended on November 11, 1918.

When Marie died, she was buried near Pierre in the small French village where he had grown up.

The fame of the great Curie family didn't end there. The very next year, Irene and Frederic Joliot-Curie were given the Nobel Prize for their own discoveries in chemistry.

Irene and Frederic had two children, Helene and Pierre. They both grew up to be scientists as well. Amazingly, Helene married Paul Langevin's grandson, who was also a scientist!

Marie's younger daughter, Eve, wasn't a scientist. She became a writer instead. She wrote a book about her mother called *Madame Curie*. Her book helped make Marie famous in America.

Marie remains the most famous woman in science, even today.

Buildings have been named after her. Two museums are devoted to her life and work. Her picture has been used on money in France and Poland.

In 1995, France decided to dig up Marie's and Pierre's caskets and move them to the Panthéon. The Panthéon is an ancient building in Paris where France's most famous people are buried. The president of France came for the big ceremony.

At last, it didn't matter that Marie Curie had been a woman. She finally was given the highest possible respect and the honor she had always deserved. Her work had changed the world, and her name would live on forever.

Timeline of Marie Curie's Life

1867	Maria Sklodowska is born in Poland.
1883	Graduates first in her high-school class at age fifteen.
1891	Arrives in Paris to attend the Sorbonne.
1895	Marries Pierre Curie.
1897	Her first daughter, Irene, is born.
1898	Discovers two new chemical elements.
1902	Obtains a sample of pure radium.
1903	Wins the Nobel Prize with Pierre for their work with radioactivity.
1904	Pierre begins teaching at the Sorbonne.
	Her second daughter, Eve, is born.
1906	Pierre is killed in an accident.
	Takes over Pierre's teaching job at the Sorbonne.
1911	Wins her second Nobel Prize.
1914	Invents an X-ray machine to help wounded soldiers on the battlefield during World War I.
1926	Daughter Irene marries Frederic Joliot.
1934	Dies at the age of sixty-six.

Timeline of the World

1863	The first passenger subway opens in London.
1865	President Abraham Lincoln is assassinated.
1869	The Suez Canal opens.
1876	Alexander Graham Bell invents the telephone.
1883	The Brooklyn Bridge opens after over a decade of construction.
1903	One of the first silent movies, *The Great Train Robbery,* premieres.
	The Wright brothers fly the first airplane.
1908	Henry Ford introduces the Model T.
1912	The *Titanic* sinks.
1914	World War I begins in Europe.
	The Panama Canal opens.
1917	The United States enters World War I.
1919	The Treaty of Versailles ends World War I.
1929	US stock market crashes, initiating the Great Depression.
1931	The Empire State Building is completed.
1932	Amelia Earhart becomes the first woman to fly solo across the Atlantic Ocean.

Bibliography

*Cobb, Vicki. Marie Curie. New York: DK Publishing, 2008.

Curie, Eve. Madame Curie: A Biography. Boston: Da Capo Press, 1937.

Goldsmith, Barbara. Obsessive Genius: The Inner World of Marie Curie. New York: Atlas Books, 2005.

Quinn, Susan. Marie Curie: A Life. Boston: Da Capo Press, 1995.

*Books for young readers